Prayers Of the Shaman

Karolyn Redonte

Plain View Press
P.O. 42255
Austin, TX 78704

plainviewpress.net
pk@plainviewpress.net
512-441-2452

Copyright © 2011 Karolyn Redoute. All rights reserved under International and Pan-American Copyright Conventions. No part of this book may be reproduced or distributed in any form or by any means, or stored in a data base or retrieval system, without written permission from the author. All rights, including electronic, are reserved by the author and publisher.

ISBN: 978-1-935514-10-7
Library of Congress Number: 2001012345

Cover image: *The Mei-Pei Lake* by Beth Ames Swartz
Author photograph: Bonnie Brabson
Cover design: Susan Bright

Acknowledgments

The following poems have been published previously: "Drowning On a Farm," *Comstock Review*, Sp/Sum 2009; "Disappearance Of the Shaman, IV," *http://seastories/hibernal 109/ Blue Ocean org*; "Shamanic Dancer," *Earth's Daughters*, 2008; "Petroglyph," *Thema*, Autumn, 2007; "Osip Mandelstam, A Transit Camp, 1938," *Many Mountains Moving*, 2006; "Ghosts On Cumberland," *Runes*, Winter 2004; "Morning, Waimanalo Bay," *Mid-America Review*, Spring 2004; "The Survivor's Loss Of an Elegy….," *Poetica, Reflections of Jewish Thought*, March 2004; "Floating," *Earth's Daughters*, 2003; "The Healing Tree," *Lifeboat, A Journal of Memoir*, Autumn 2003; "Prayers Of the Shaman I, II and III" and "Bones Of the Wolf," *Sophie's Wind*, Fall 2000; "The Glassmaker," *Common Lives, Lesbian Lives*, Fall 1994. The author would also like to thank Sharon Doubiago, Sherry Quan Lee and the Split Rock Arts Program for support in completion of this manuscript.

The refuge given by the wind is the helplessness at the core of prayer.

Coleman Barks, *The Soul of Rumi*

Contents

Spirit   9

    Bones Of the Wolf   11
    Ghosts On Cumberland   12
    The Disappearance Of the Shaman   13
    Grief   16
    Prophecy Of the Shaman   17
    A Psychic Urging a Memory   18

Prayer   21

    Prayers Of the Shaman   23
    Fourth Prayer Of the Shaman   25
    Fifth Prayer Of the Shaman   26
    Petroglyph   27

Grief   29

    Morning, Waimanalo Bay   31
    Going Back East Out Of Angelus, Kansas   32
    On Talking To a Student With Aniridia   33
    Before a Storm   35
    White Cloth   36
    The Bearer Of Rain   37

Earth   39

    Floating   41
    The Door   42
    Refugee   43
    Wild Russian Olive   44
    Our Yard As the Sanctuary Of Apollo   45
    Unwritten Myths   46
    Family Grief   50

Ice   53

    Osip Mandelstam   55
    The End Of the Desert   58
    The Ice Child   59

Myth   65

    The Spell Unbroken   67
    Drowning On a Farm   68
    Witness   69
    Penelope In Present Time   70

Promise   71

    The Glassmaker   73
    Shamanic Dancer   74
    The Fate Of the Net   75
    The Healing Tree   77
    Denial Of a Myth   78
    Trust   80
    Georgia O'Keefe/ Sanctuary Of Blue   81

Voice   85

    Broken Lines   87
    Desert Story   88
    The Survivor's Loss Of an Elegy For the Night Of Fire   90

    About the Author   93

*For Linda Alis, Dwight Noble,
and for Jennifer Moore*

Spirit

Bones Of the Wolf

wolf child   I died
in the blue desert
a buried flower
and now I am glass

unbury me   I am blue with cold
I dream now in the earth
but in my dreams I travel

making things that shudder
and knock in the wind
so you might hear me

I know you think I have died
and have no heart so you cease
to follow me   but I am still
here and dream
the best I can

of cold   how the white moon
changes at certain latitudes
the beauty of mock moons
jagged ice   drifted snow
prisms of ice
across a zenith

I have dreamed these into art

but there is just so much time
my body can dream
in this drifting place

read my glass heart
unbury me

Ghosts On Cumberland

storm-dark crown of an island tree   mane
of a horse thrashing at the bridle   clatter of hoofs
woman in dust   wailing at sunrise   her child
stolen like the moon

she searches for the boy slave   gone from his tree
-carved cradle   the deep chasm of her belly
empty   of the sound of his cries

men and women picking figs and pomegranates
hear her cry aside the rows   in her mind
gourds fly in the wind   drums shake
shellbones rattle on the sea

her voice is wild above the foamy brine
sandpiper and plover   a whirl of salt
rolls through her thighs

her braids fly like clouds   in the red-dyed sky
the waves pound her knees   wild to the ship
rocking on wind   she raving   like wings
at the crow's nest

a blue stone bead sinks to the sand
below her splayed feet
a charm   they say   against evil

The Disappearance Of the Shaman

white hoof prints
hold the weight of snow
I bend
to the shallows
of a bone and hear
the jagged rhythm
of a heart
abandoned
on the plain

I dream again
my ear against blue
bone shadow
resting on
the snowy earth
I try to bring
the body back to life
and fail

as I rise
I turn to see
white beasts walking
all around me
in slow motion
towards a place
of prayer

caribou walk
through my body
as if I was not there

O

my heart flies out
of my breastbone
and escapes
into the larch

my heart is an injured falcon
taking cover
clutching branches
hanging on
waiting for the wind

○

if I disappear
the hawk
flies free

○

I am the ash
of a dying star and the fire
of a new one
my blood is the red stain
on a far away moon
my eyes look out
from ice where
I kneel before the fox
on earth as white
as bloodless skin

if I go away
into the dark
the animal
will live

○

I sleep in the dead bones
of the humpback
amid the dark
moon craters
of the ocean floor

    the notes of her singing
      are stranded now
     in the ear bones of
         her kin
         melodies
    that skeletons carry
         in water

Grief

black bird flies out of your heart
you are not sure where it is going
or why it is leaving
it rises into the blackest night
where still there are no stars

you walk the jagged earth
over mountains to lose
mother and father   each step
burying them again
your steps criss-cross in grief
there is no easy way to leave
a mother or a father
behind

tired at the end of the journey
you lean closer to the sky
and the sky befriends you
and you can bow your head
to hear the words

yet as you look down
there is no book of prayer
that will comfort
your eyes try to speak
but fail in the quiet

then your soul does all
the singing   sings all night
if it can   songs
of another world

it is the black bird
flying out of the heart
not sure where it is going
it is the hollow cave restless
with the echo of wings

Prophecy Of the Shaman

souls

written in shadow

where wolf moved   winds

where hawk slept   moons

where raven sang   hollows

where fox lay   dreams

of animals sing all night

in my hands   come

back to life

each morning

many moons it takes

many suns   to bring back souls

A Psychic Urging a Memory

*Beneath your backbone I can feel
a tree shedding its skin
in ribbons of light,*

*slender leaves of a willow
winding along a riverbank,
tracks on the silent ground*

*close to a hayfield,
footsteps moving
through long grass and*

*the wind in the rolling hills
confused sheep
flocking toward the barn*

*a barn not far
from wild deep stones,
maybe a river moving red*

*with clouds
near an empty road,
the soft underwing*

*of a heron
marking the air
like a messenger with no address*

    you have the body of a woman
    but I see the soul of a man
    hidden like a ghost

    in your girlish bones
    the ghost of a colored man
    the itinerant field hand

who smiled at you one morning
and played with you
and was kind

later he would understand
that he was not allowed to smile
at you or your sisters

your muscles are taut
with a memory
of his face

I can see your grandfather
pushing you into a wooden
box   so that you wouldn't see

the knife or his field hands
circling Thomas Brothers
in the hayloft   in revenge

the old man gave the signal
you heard his voice   the scuttling feet
the leaping cry   the fall

then silence   and after
they dragged you out of the box
and you saw the body lying

on the floor   parts of you sailed away
like clouds   and your psyche split
apart the moon hanging in the window

of the barn   I watch the soiled curtain
shrouding your heart   I can feel the air
above it and below   I can see

his fallen body in your nerves
and blood   how you keep
his vigil like a child

waiting in the dark for a sound
I hear the guilty voices saying
you were the cause of the death

others whisper of your innocence
and his   voices sing back and forth
inside your head because you are alone

in what you now recall   yes   you grew up
around men who went fishing and sang
in the church choir and ate at the table

like anybody else   so no wonder child
your memory wonders of such secret crime
now the soul of the fallen man is rising up

in waves of light speaking to my skin   listen
child   I beg of you   hear his shining light
in mercy for you both   hear his shining light

beneath my outspread hand

Prayer

Prayers Of the Shaman

I bless
the winding plains
I am nowhere

I follow wild horses
home at the end of the day
a home within the air

I breathe the wild dust
on the blue plains

my hoofs of air

run through mountains
and out again leaving
surges of dust no one
can follow

all my prayers move
through pain and heal
like the wind
moves
through mountains

like the wind

○

I unfold my feathered arms and my heart
talks to the wind in the grass   I bow
to the bones in the gray earth and die
in the hollow of my body

I am interloper gypsy vagrant spy
stealing the country of wind   and when I come
back from the deep earth   I make
prayers of the air

my heart is a mystery

I fly with your deepest desire

follow me   believe in
my dance

my hands enfolding
the diamond
lodged
in your breastbone

like a book
of wisdom or song

○

I have broken glass
wherever I have lived
the veins of white
follow me like broken strands
of hair in icy water

the glass has watched me each time
I bring the dead back to life

but each time
my reflection breaks I
have fewer pieces
of the moon
to eat

who will learn
my secrets   if the moon
abandons me
my children die
and I no longer dream

Fourth Prayer Of the Shaman

shaman looks up
knife falls
spire of ice   spirits
in my eyes
shaman becomes two
loses face
becomes another

dead salmon   black eye
open mouth   floating belly up
silver yellow drifting
moons

who am I   shaman who is lost
who am I   ancient blessings
no good now
walking stick with bells
no one hears

water   grass   smelly wind
I go behind my coat
of water and enter
a doorway
made of death
and the deathwind takes me
down a river

my heart is slow
it drifts into grass
and falls on
slippery brown
stones

like salmon
I am here   I am moving
but I am disappearing

Fifth Prayer Of the Shaman

weeds blowing
clouds walking
on land and forever

each time it is cut
the earth hardens
like a heart

the hand is woven
with rope
the throat shuts
tight

I speak from the trees
from a noose
in the clouds
looking down
at earth
searching

for medicine
branch   flower   leaf
I know

the sky can cure
with its vast wind

the land is like a book
with the pages torn

the sky
is like the healing

Petroglyph

Prairie town, evening.

Out of the smoky garage
a uniformed mechanic emerges. On his frayed cap
above the visor, the insignia torn, dark pinholes
hang in the shape of a diamond and arrow,
a lost constellation of stars.

She asks him for directions.

"Two lefts, then a ways down the road," he says,
and disappears behind a door in the dark.

◯

The road seems endless, more and more
corn. Waving grass, one cross-
road, then another. She begins to doubt
the mechanic. Wants to turn back
to confront him with a map, until

the cardboard buffalo appears, and the sign
that shows the ancient Indian stones.
She looks back down the road
no longer visible in the sun.

Was he only an imaginary angel?
Did she know the path all along?

That isn't easy to answer.

◯

Farther down the road, stones
lie in the earth
like the backs of ancient
animals rising from the deep,

scars on their backs,
stories, some say.

○

The Lakota, even now, come here
to pray. They trust the stones. They have always trusted
the whereabouts of rock.

This is how the prairie prays,
in mystery. That is why

the rocks
take so long
to find.

○

If you wish to learn
how to pray,
take a prairie road.

Grief

Morning, Waimanalo Bay

In the distance golden rock glinting
in steam. The body of a woman
sculpting the water in mist,
her palms a white-yellow flame.

The sun burns blue in the shallows.
Milk fish scatter. Two golden plovers
peck holes in the wash of the tide.
Spokes of driftwood fan across

white sand. I hear the *apapane*
hiding in eucalyptus, the rock dove
invisible in palms. I watch
the swimmer disappear

like a star before daybreak,
searching for her, certain that her body
hangs poised in blue fire,
like starlight.

Going Back East Out Of Angelus, Kansas

The rolling hills of western Kansas.
Blue swallows circle a blackened steeple
empty of bells. The ghosts of farmers
wander the fields at night till daybreak,
then again at noon. You can hear
the tall grasses whisper of the loss,
of prayers no longer said.

A purple columbine torn on a wire fence.
The collar of a woman's silken blouse fading
on a line of clothes. Your body washed
in indigo, a shadow walking an empty street
between the gun shop and the sad hotel.
The loss of love in your eyes echoes

deeper now, as you drive past Highway 63,
through lonely corn fields,
pastures of bluegrass,
and fields with fallen dogwood
farther south.

On Talking To a Student With Aniridia

Looking away from the golden
wheat fields, the green cypress
and white clouds rolling
above a blue steeple
framed on my office wall,

I enter instead the dark

archways of a monastery
deep with cellars,
and absent of swallows,
her eyes. I look towards her
as I would a solitary oak,

the only tree standing for miles,

though she sits before me
in the chair, refusing
to think of herself as an oak
or an archway, refusing
to be beautiful

in her darkness. It is difficult

to believe in beauty
without light, to go deeply
into the soul bathed in gray,
yet all of us must,
when we enter a solitude,

a loneliness.

She looks down toward the floor,
shoulders sloping, her dark eyes
sway inward like willows

by the water's edge
at midnight. Gently, regretfully,

she says, "*I can't finish school.*"

○

The words are meant to keep me
away, and yet to keep me near.
They beckon me to enter
the darkness, the deep passage
where she waits, ready to flee.

We both wait in the silence then,

for a long while, until quietly
I take a small step,
and enter what I think
is a fortress, full of stone
and weight, and walk instead

through a delicate archway

where I see her running
in the wind, near wheat fields
deep with cypress, whose colors
in the long twilight, I strain,
and struggle, to see.

"Anridia" means "absence, or partial absence, of the iris."

Before a Storm

when your eyelids
close   the wind rushes
away the tangled manes
of the blind island ponies
their hooves write
a calligraphy   lost
on the sandy path
through darkened woods

in the morning snowy
egrets fly upward
and vanish   the ponies hide
quietly in the fields

you can hear their soft
breath in the shadows

White Cloth

my heart patched in divisions
like the canvas sail of a junket ship
my breath struggling through the sheath
the threads someone else has sewn

if only I could write what I am feeling on the cloth
and send it to you through the billowing air
and you could write back to me on the other side
your hope for what could be

healing passes through white cloth   your love
would be like healing

The Bearer Of Rain

in a dream
I carry a small bamboo boat
along a northern shore
I am not sure
what keeps me from floating
the hull onto water

fear of the rolling clouds
or thoughts of what
the vessel once contained
it begins to rain   I shift

and the boat fills
slowly with water
I struggle
to hold the lapping water

but soon my shoulders sink
into the clay-like sand
I cannot raise
my body toward the sky

as day breaks the waves
begin to chant   their tongues
dark and cold
I begin to see

the boat that I had carried
through my waking
was broken   charred
and empty

I wonder what fire
I carried from another life
into this one   what emptiness
I tried to fill
with rain

Earth

Floating

My mother, after her stroke, found you
in a dream, her voice filtered through
the wind of a rainstorm.   It happened
the night she was on morphine

500 miles away, her femur
fractured just below the hip, her hands
folding imaginary clothes, searching
for shelves out of reach.

I could see my mother standing
by the hallway with the laundry
in her arms and then again
in the doorway of the cottage

on Lake Erie, her aged body
40 years younger, her blue and orange
housecoat blossoming on a body
supple and lithe, like the stem

of a hollyhock in summer.
She leaned against the doorjamb, hip
to wood, her long legs willowy
and slanted toward the side,

her feet shoeless, like a young girl.
I remember she nearly lost
her balance that day, and
for a moment she was

almost floating, like the silvery light
after the morning rain
that hangs on the leaves
of the beech trees.

The Door

in my dream the scuffed oak door of our house
hangs in the clouds
hammered steel handle in the shape
of a question mark
small windows full of sky

I see my mother   much younger   hesitating
in the old sedan   unsure
if the house is locked   she runs back
to the porch steps   clutching a key
and freezes

in my dream
the door is not there

when I wake
I remember

that after my aging parents fled
the neighborhood our small house
became a den for crack and was set on fire
the door burned from the fire

I realized that all the disaster
that my mother feared
happened *then*   that all her worry
could not prevent

this dreaded end   her hastening back
to the house was a deep foretelling
over and over again

a grief
of losing all
she had

Refugee

When my mother was a child, she refused food,
after spells of choking. About the time
her own mother was dying from TB
in another town.

I think of the refugee children getting off a train
in Prague after World War II, a war of her generation:
the small starved bodies gorging themselves
on rice, their stomachs forgetting
how to take in food. I see my mother
as a refugee from that hollow place

of childhood where there is loss
that never gets explained.
I see her boarding a train, after her father's death,
watching the snow cover the houses in small
towns. A girl losing her family,
going on, like any refugee.

Now my mother lies on a hospital bed,
her own children grown. It is May. I notice
how her joints jut out at the elbow and the wrist,
how her blouse rises and falls like paper
on a wave. She tells me that yesterday she traveled
to her childhood home. When I offer
her a slice of apple from a spoon,
she stares across the room. I know she has forgotten
who I am. In her eyes

I see the color of a winter sky at sea,
a parched, war-torn land.
I meet her gaze, where she looks at me,
from the window of a passing train.

Wild Russian Olive

In a former incantation she watched tender white blossoms
floating from slender leaves onto the breaking sea,
her tears burning with the bittersweet scent of the wild olive.
A sailor held her close, then fled the wind-swept town
and rowed away. On the street now she mumbles to herself,
an old immigrant woman with a cane. When the wind passes
through her bones, she knows she's been loved in another life, somehow
loved. Under the canopy of silvery green which she passes,
the shredding bark and falling yellow berries reveal nothing
of her life: a sailor's disappearance, starvation in the steppe, souls
at work in some gulag. As she limps by, she brags out loud about
her kitchen on the boulevard in old Detroit, and then decries
the sulfurous stink of the factory on the River Rouge, where
her husband poured molten steel night after night into fiery vats. She
spits once at the vodka on his breath, and then pauses
for the morning breeze, as it floats over the lawns. Tonight she will
sit by the fire, drink caravan tea, and dream
of silver trees.

Our Yard As the Sanctuary Of Apollo

He tilted the brown bottle
over the river rock. The rock foamed.
He dragged his feet through the flower bed,
slurring cuss words and stumbling
near the rose bed. He fell

between the thorns. If only the flood-
light had found him then, challenging
him to speak. He could have raised his face,
mask-like, to heaven, and been transformed.

If only she had gotten work
as a sibyl, she could have gathered
dandelions into swaths of laurel leaf
and pots of fake flowers into bowls
of steaming revelations. If only
she had realized her gifts
of intuition, perhaps she would have

confronted him where he lay
face down amid the rose thorns
and the stones, and offered him
some imperative to change the course
of fate. If only our house
had stood near the dreamy oily
limestone faults that whispered
to the oracle the aromas of divinity.
If only.

Unwritten Myths

After my sister and I were born,
both my parents created myths.

It began when my mother observed
my father standing in the yard

behind the a-frame house,
conversing with the birds.

Holding handfuls of seed,
he said, "*At times I feel*

I am St. Francis." She began
to make myths about this scene

in her disbelief: he was nervous,
overworked, needed to birdwatch

as a hobby. My father's myths
unfortunately continued.

One day he told my mother
that he suspected his boss

was poisoning his coffee.
Complaints of unspecific

ailments continued, and so
did the blessing of the birds.

My mother described how
eventually she got my father

to St. Joseph's, a retreat
hospital formerly for priests

in the suburbs of Detroit.
When they came to take him

from the bungalow, he told her,
"I'll be going to the monastery now."

○

St. Joseph's was run by The Sisters of Charity,
brilliant with light in their winged bonnets.

They walked happily from room to room,
white linen draped over their dutiful

arms. Apparently my father walked
the hallways too, attempting

to speak to the statues, most often to
St. Joseph, patron saint of fathers.

For me these conversations
will be forever lost in mystery,

like the mythic ones
he had with birds.

○

Perhaps it was a childhood grief
too unbearable to slay

that made him talk
to phantoms: the green-scaled tail

and the breathing fire lurking
invisible within. In the days

of St. George there were magical
beasts who embodied pain.

As a child my father had no help
in slaying these. As years passed,

the sad dragons of his childhood
must have waited

within him, anxious to roar,
longing in their lairs to find a name,

or an anodyne for pain. When
his battles ended, and his reason fled,

he found brief refuge
among the robins in our yard.

Who knows if my father ever saw
the caves of fire lurking

in his past, or subdued them
with his prayer?

                    ○

After six weeks he returned
home, defeated, silent

and withdrawn, healed by jolts
from wires, not by Heaven's light.

Charity had its limits. For a while
my father gazed at us like a wounded beast

unable to roam or fly. It was a summer
early in my childhood and my sister's.

I did not understand it then,
but I remember. I hear

the family story now, as I begin
to learn my own unwritten myths.

Family Grief

A two-tone, cream and pink '59 Chevy.
My mother in the driver's seat, but facing us,
her back to the road, the wheel behind her nearly still.
The car moves slowly, as if in a cortege. An arch of branch
and leaf shadow the car. It is almost night, but the road
is stony white. She doesn't seem to notice where we are
or how the car is barely moving.

She speaks to us about our father, her graceful hands
moving through the missing steering wheel.
My sister listens without offering advice.
I anxiously scan the windshield,
half hearing my mother's tears,
the old staging of the drama
of my father's life: from childhood,
to war, to drink. We move
under a deeper canopy and deeper

into shadow, until suddenly,
my mother's hands are old and veined
and very still. In the dark her wedding ring
and necklace glisten
like moonlight on a lake.

I pray with my sister
for grace to fill the silence.
The car continues down
the road without a driver.

○

My father sits behind the wheel
of the white Impala. He has worked too many
night shifts in parcel post. He drives past
the signs by the lift bridge
and into the sky. My sister stares out the windshield

as we hang above the water. All of us wait,
like drifting geese in clouds
searching the darkness for the road.

○

I sit in a car on a street I don't know.
The steering column cover falls apart.
I look into the rear-view mirror. The glass is
blank. The car feels light, suddenly,
as if the engine on its own had taken flight.
The transmission shifts like a rising wave,

yet I am still, paralyzed
on the ground, alone.
I wait to hear an argument
between my parents
about which road to take.
Like a child I wonder
if the anger will finally start
the engine of the car.
Nothing happens,
as I turn my hand holding a key
that isn't there.
I hope for some direction, even
an impatient horn.

There is no sound. The seasons
change. Snow falls
on my hair and on
my eyelids through a broken window.

I cannot find my sister.

I long, on waking, to ask
the road a question,

but instead keep on schedule
on my way to work,
passing the accidents, forgetting

the dreams, the time it takes
to grieve the deaths
of parents.

Ice

Osip Mandelstam

A Transit Camp, Siberia, 1938

crystal fog
pink snow on the ice fields
in the night

I dream of elm leaves pulsing
with color in the trees
I reach for them

the leaves
become white rags
I try to sew

the leaves into pages
but the slender threads
fall away from my hands

I look for a way to find ink
from red berries but the *oblepikha*
bush bleeds in my fingers

now neither hand can write
a rough-legged hawk
flies overhead

the pale wing beats fade
into clouds and when I wake
I write this in my mind

I memorize the ice fields
at the faint sound of my heart
I recall the razor in my shoe

but fail to use it
I think of the hope my wife has
the hope in silent words

○

am I real and
will death
ever come

it is easier to taste
the pale bread
of paper than the heavy

blood of ink
if I write in short breaths
unlike I used to

it is because
I count more
moments than hours

more hours than days
of someone else's hope
Forgive me

○

for what I am
telling you　some day
my words will come

to you in snow   the unwritten ones
you will transcribe them
in the bleak sun

of your own winter   we are alike
fast in our chain links   our secrets
I predict my voice

will come to you on the days
when you lose heart and need
a witness most   you may find only

a faint placing of words
forgive me
my mind must be the paper now

but come back for me
imaginary scribe
tell all about the fields

returning in the vast spring
with the rowan and the larch
and the flowers of every color

The End Of the Desert

> On *Passages*, a film by Shirin Neshat/Philip Glass

my hands are white with dust from digging
in the earth   men carry a body
in procession   across the horizon by the sea
but I do not look up

my hands are turning white like paper
but I have forgotten how to write
I have stopped imagining
my face or the loving face
of any other

I bow my head and the dust washes
away whatever I see in the distance
this tireless abyss
in the ground could be a fountain
offering me diamonds
from its flumes   a mirage of diamonds
I would have to dig forever

for the dust to clear   to know
sometimes I still believe
in the purpose of our journey   though
my knees beg the earth for time
and my hands lie empty
from grasping   what only falls away

the desert is white like paper where nothing
is written   like the morning sky
I cannot raise my face to see

The Ice Child

buried words under snow
words I no longer know

when I try to search for them
it is like finding
a prayer book
no one has opened

a prayer book made of snow

who are you

*there is no way you can know
of me except
to write of snow*

tell me who you are

*a voice
my words are scavengers
that hunt you in the night
under the aurora, the west wind
the smiling sun of childhood*

O

I can't imagine why you've come

yes you can

*but I see you do not know how
to talk to me, I who sleep inside of you*

*I have appeared because
you must learn
to use words of ice
and cold and waiting*

*now you cannot write the book
of your life directly or reveal
the pain on white pages
the pain you do not want*

○

to know as your own

*I am your ice child, the being
you have silenced
so well within you: I am neither child nor woman
and I am both/ I am fragile,
like crystalline,
and may break like ice, at the sound
of my true name*

○

*I had a doll once who was buried
in my memory
year after year she lives
in a floating place where I lost her
on a sidewalk of snow
she is the only ice child I know*

*she still lives—
in the secret story
of the ice, as I do*

*how often you pretend
we don't exist
write down my words of ice*

*if you don't, I must
find still another wizard or witch
doctor who specializes in snow
to tell you all of the story*

how can I write of a voice I hardly know

*listen to my mysteries
if I offer
you a half-made life, I am sorry

so many nights
when I wish to move I only become snow
there is no book of my life within you yet
for when it is hard to read
the book of snow
you do not try
I know when you look in the mirror, I
turn to long white fields
you try to see me out the white
window, but I am hidden
as white as a clavicle
a shinbone or driftwood

you forget me, believing I am lost, yet
slow rhythms of the snow world enfold me
in the dark
if I speak this way so often
of cold, it because I want you

to do nothing but listen
for once in your life
I want you to find me*

○

    in the deepest cold

one day my eyes went icy blue
like marbles of watery salt
I must have cried
for the loss
of my doll

hear me
read the ice flowers
I have drawn
they are pieces of your story

little ridges of snow
and salt pressed
against the ice

if you put your hand
into the print of the flower
you will see that I live
in the places in your body you ignore
your white breath your white muscle your white bone
leg stomach lung skin
I am
all you refuse to feel
and all you deny

the land where I live is
asleep like a memory

the words of the story
always turn to snow

○

write the words in ice
so that I might know:

the moon
passing across the sky
white birds as blinding as snow
I am
forced to swallow
saltwater and blood,
red as starfish, at the edge
of my bed,
this is the half-told
story that hangs in me
like ice

I live in a cradle
of ice where you have left
me for nearly a lifetime

sometimes I remember
how it was
in the house of my childhood:

the blinding moon of light
in the hallway, the white sleeves
of my father's shirt, his arms
flashing suddenly like the beating
wings of hundred of wild birds
my teeth clenched
in my mouth wet with salt

○

*will you know where
to find me in the white night?
I am the ice child
buried in snow
I am your memory*

Myth

The Spell Unbroken

More often the beast is never kissed. His story becomes a secret.
In spite of his insolent girth, his one eye and heavy tusks, he finds
a way to marry, perhaps a woman unaware of beauty, or what it means
to be wakened by a kiss.

After they have a child, the wife of the beast sleepwalks
through the hallways of their nights, an enchanted book closed shut
within her arms. Unable to sleep, her husband also roams
the house, passing all the mirrors, staring out the doorways
at the moon. Long a prisoner of time, and longing,
the beast with thorny head and whiskered cheek pauses often
at his daughter's room. One night he tells the little girl his secret,
seeking the magic kiss from her.

As the years go by, the child forgets the kiss,
and the enchantment of her father, and the meaning
of his story. As if enchanted too, she roams the world
in search of Beauty, of becoming Beauty,
but sadly, does not find her.

Drowning On a Farm

you heard the command to kneel
before the pig trough   felt the pulling down

the roots of your hair   the shame at your throat
what crime had you committed   you screamed

then without warning he submerged your head
until the shadow of the sun became your face

and your face the cold dark
water   you heard the faint

flapping of wings of the herons
flying overhead over

a land that was already lost
you prayed to see the sky again

he waited and relented
full of curses but by then

you stopped believing in the sky
part of you passed away into oblivion

no wonder after so many years
no one can tell you

you are beautiful
and be believed   you look away

your eyes full of dark bracken
and lonely birds   and breathless

as if the water
hung there like a veil

Witness

Your sleeping hand touches your forehead. I watch
how your hand falls again, breath by breath,
to your heart. Turning, you ask me to come
into your dream as a witness.   I already believe

that we have arrived at the hayfield
and that you will wait, unable to make
a sound. Your seven-year old eyes fight
tears as your grandmother ties
your body to a fence post
in the midnight fields. The coils of rope burn
through your chest, your arms and legs
fall limp. When you finally open
your eyes, you hear the old woman
muttering "temptress"
beyond the trees.

How could anyone imagine
your grandmother's hands
flying like the wings of crows, the rope
spinning like a snake, the endless
wooden fence holding back the stars?
Perhaps you still believe
only the deep night sky can hear
your wishes to be saved
from passing cars on state road 46,

yet how often have I watched your arms
fling off the rope in sleep, as you try
to return to the child, her eyes searching
the poplars and the oaks,
the fields of hay, for a witness.

Penelope In Present Time

Black and white, night and day, endless
on the horizon. All that he is invisible.
I steer his ship through a telepathic haze.
As I weave, my arms cross my heart and cover it.
No one will learn the stories I create. My heart is
constantly moving in the dark. Some nights
I see monsters like a sibyl, but weave them into art.
A thousand men could not help me un-change the
weaving with the day.

A woman waiting learns the fallacy
of expectation early, how never to count on words
to end a story. I weave the yarns without worry
of a beginning, or an end, or any unexpected turn
of fate. The monotony of vigilance
has taught me to rely on intuition, for the mystery
of its comfort, and my hands take it into infinity,
defying time. Instructed by a net of longings
the object of my desire will never know

in present time, diligence drives my art.
Weaving with no care of outcomes,
I make his journey come to life. Unswerving,
I create a story with accidental turns
and mistaken endings. In the finishing
my art will become eternal
myth its artist never intentionally imagined,
except in the making and unmaking
of the threads. In this way I steer the ship
and take his journey home.

Promise

The Glassmaker

Each night the shadow
of the desert moon falls
through the circle
of my adobe roof.

When I unbraid my hair,
diamonds
fall like stars
from the shadow.

If you have lost your way
in the black night,
I will wait for you,

and breathe the broken
fire into glass
as smooth as a woman's body
rising and curving
in her lover's arms.

Shamanic Dancer

small rib bones
of the garden snake
tiny as baby teeth
inside your hand

shake them into life
they dance   with spirit
throw them back
to earth   they fall

like a child's dice
on the prairie ground
I will go this way
when I go

dancing down   dancing in
the grasses dancing in
the stillness
of the wind

The Fate Of the Net

you push her away with your eyes   taking pains
to avoid her as you sway back
and forth   her eyes move with you
her soul full of prayer

she watches you as you make love
to the fake and distant stars
painted on the circus tent   silent
recalcitrant

you reach for the swinging bar   just in time
and the arm of the strongman clown
catches you up above
again   you look away

from the beautiful goddess
you sleep with
only by accident
she is accustomed to this

distance   ever vigilant she knows
it is because of her
that you can fly   and yet her soul
is what sustains you most

the sleeping angel who watches
under you   and over you
though you look down
at her with dread

is above all longing of the flesh
if she dreams of a time
when she might wake
with you close   it is only

when she closes her eyes
the house lights
are out and you are not there
in the dark world of dreams   she knows

when you climb the ladder to the stars
encircled by the crowds   she is the bearer
of your fate   the one who needs
you least   and most of all

The Healing Tree

When I was a child,
after arguments at dinner,
I went out to the yard
and wounded the apple tree.
I took a toy tomahawk
and cut a deeper gash
each night until the bone
of the tree was visible.

Sometimes when I was older,
I would notice the spreading
arms and the gash at the heart
of the tree and look away,
not wanting to remember
the wound. Only now,
since the house
and yard have been sold,

have I been dreaming
of apple blossoms
falling through the glass
of my window at night.
There is no end
to their falling,
their gentle
spreading down.

Denial Of a Myth

on the black river the boatman
rows through moonlight   his oars
luminous in the summer night
in his wake

a wriggling fish disappears
like strands of silver tissue
into water   the dark waves
move around his boat

through a mysterious
alchemy and reach
the river's edge transfixed
in light   those on shore

move blindly in the dark
the scent of bitter lilies
faint   like a heartbeat
or a breath

seeing the boatman
the stranded travelers
throw coins hoping
for a passage out   a sheen

of silver falls through
the air like rain   the glittering
coins hang briefly in the air
then disappear

into the dark water
at dawn   the boatman
rows towards shore
and calls out

the names of the islanders
the sounds echo
off the chalky cliffs   as the oars
of his boat touch shore

○

*There's a myth about death they used to tell
about this river, but nobody wrote it down,
and it would only be the island of money trees
spangling by the deep river beds, the wind shaking,
the wild silver trout disappearing
into the undertow and the white limestone cliffs reflecting
shadows on the rock*

*there is no light transforming the river now
since it is almost winter; no one,
and nothing, moves through the light in winter,
no rowboat or rower ever comes,
and no one waits, at call of crow,
for passage, any time of year*

Trust

and I believed them
as you would believe the rain

doves in the eaves
which my father said

always promised rain
and the moon

the golden rings
of mist around it

all those things
that promised rain

it has taken me years
to trust the weather

without thinking
of my father

Georgia O'Keefe/ Sanctuary Of Blue

through an archway
of light

a flower falls
by a bleached bone

in a flotation
of clouds

the sky hinges
on the wings

of a ram's horn
and the strange
happiness

of a white
hollyhock
also floating

in sky

you enter
plains of hill
and sand

waves
of gray
and vermillion

shadows
of white
cliff and ridge

a woman
like
a cloud

holds you
with her eyes
all morning

you watch
black lightning
turning inward

or a wild black-
eyed flower
hovering

above pink foothills
a pale dry
silence

at your lips
you see her
spirit also winds

and shifts
through cedars
marked with

the blooddust
of white bone
her body

becomes
a sanctuary
of blue

as you learn
to love
her music

pale sky and snaking tree
stark cross

swaying jimson weed
lily rushing red

everything that moves
in sacred air

Voice

Broken Lines

voices come from journeys
I take to escape
a life that is barely mine
the words I gather together here
come from useless shards

that is how the shaman sings
fragments first   and then belief

Desert Story

you lose your way
in the blue cold   the blue wind
traveling to empty places
pursuing what is useless
to your art

others by now
have told their stories
while you wake in exile
nothing published of your life
and sometimes in your eyes
it is as if
you haven't lived

it isn't true

begin to tell the story
of the desert again
with random words from a notebook
saguaro and moon
joshua tree
loss
mesquite seed
desert willow   love
of a woman
meadowlark

offer us fragments on scattered paper
the wild land abides by
its own grace and will give you back
your body   the litany within it

use the ink you stored in
dark glass bottles   the old
marble pens you never filled
with liquid

and in all your words pray
you can live

each day the desert
light will return
you to your story

The Survivor's Loss Of an Elegy For the Night Of Fire

Anselm Kiefer, *Breaking of the Vessels*, 1990

The giant leaden bindings hung
from tall metal shelves like clothes
without bodies. I saw the gray dust from fire
on mock pages shattered on the floor:
white words erased
from blackened paper shards.
The room was wreckage
transported from a distant war and left;
books and broken window glass,
half ash, carelessly strewn,
a depiction of a holy man's last hour
as he read the word of God, or the laws
of a remote city torched and left
as trash.

My eyes, the eyes of a refugee
on the street, searched the broken pieces
for a memory: the voice of hate
turning the veins in my body to glass, then
the vision of a book I had written
in secret, many times.
I recognized the black letters
as indelible as ink in skin
charred to silent gray, the cover

like an ashen coat torn
from its trembling seam.
The light darted
from page to empty page,
because I could not say
the awful truth.

But how strange, how miraculous
to have arrived here
at this hour as a witness:

my books so carefully written
have been broken over and over
with my own hands,

and yet I have survived.

About the Author

Karolyn Redoute received a B.A. in English from Wayne State University in Detroit, Michigan, and a Masters of Fine Arts in Creative Writing from Indiana University-Bloomington. She enjoys participating in the active arts community in Minneapolis, Minnesota, and leads a book group on nature and environmental issues at True Colors, an independent bookstore in town. Currently she advises and teaches students about individualized study at the University of Minnesota and is a member of the Association for the Study of Literature and the Environment.